21st Century Skills INNOVATION *Library*

Movies

by Annie Buckley

INNOVATION IN ENTERTAINMENT

Published in the United States of America by Cherry Lake Publishing
Ann Arbor, Michigan
www.cherrylakepublishing.com

Content Adviser: Tom Dowd, Professor, Columbia College Chicago

Design: The Design Lab

Photo Credits: Cover and page 3, ©JUPITER IMAGES/Creatas/Alamy; page 4, ©Rafael Ramirez
Lee, used under license from Shutterstock, Inc.; pages 6, 11, 12, and 27, ©Pictorial Press Ltd./
Alamy; page 9, ©iStockphoto.com/RapidEye; page 14, ©Jason Maehl, used under license from
Shutterstock, Inc.; pages 15 and 18, ©Classic Stock/Alamy; page 16, ©Photos 12/Alamy; page
20, ©PCL/Alamy; page 21, ©Image State/Alamy; page 23, ©AP Photo/Gina Gayle; page 25,
©AP Photo; page 28, ©AP Photo/Lucy Nicholson

Library of Congress Cataloging-in-Publication Data
Buckley, Annie.
 Movies / by Annie Buckley.
   p. cm.–(Innovation in entertainment)
 ISBN-13: 978-1-60279-222-7
 ISBN-10: 1-60279-222-4
 1. Motion pictures–Juvenile literature. 2. Cinematography–Juvenile literature. I. Title. II. Series.
 PN1994.5.B833 2009
 791.43–dc22   2008002027

Cherry Lake Publishing would like to acknowledge the work of
The Partnership for 21st Century Skills.
Please visit www.21stcenturyskills.org *for more information.*

CONTENTS

INNOVATION IN   ENTERTAINMENT

CHAPTER ONE

The Beginning of Motion Pictures

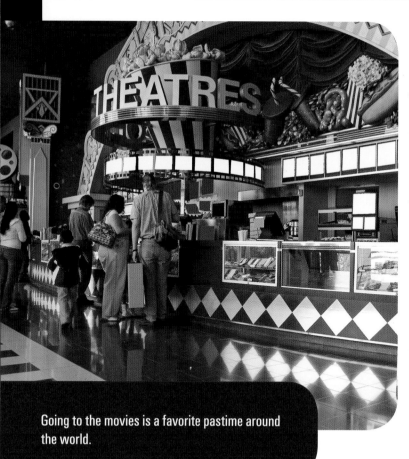

Going to the movies is a favorite pastime around the world.

Almost everyone loves going to the movies. They have the power to entertain people. But how did it all get started? Who made the first motion picture? How are movies made? How did the movie business grow to become a multi-billion dollar **industry**? It has taken a lot of innovation and creativity to make movies as popular as they are today.

Until the late 1800s, photographs were still images. Then in 1888, a man named Louis Le Prince filmed the first motion picture on a bridge in Leeds, England. Seven years later, in Paris, France, two brothers named Louis and Auguste Lumiére were the first to project a movie for a paying audience. The experience of watching a movie was almost magical. Audiences loved the new motion pictures, so the brothers took their show on the road. They sent films, projectors, and projectionists (people to show the films) to countries around the world, including Russia, India, Mexico, and Thailand.

The Lumiére brothers were not the only people creating motion pictures. New developments were made in other parts of the world. English inventor Robert William Paul developed and built cameras for filming movies. American inventor Thomas Edison became interested in movies when he saw the work of Eadweard Muybridge. Muybridge was a photographer who strung together pictures of animals in motion. Edison invented a way to move film smoothly and continuously through a movie camera. Another American, George Eastman, founder of the Kodak photography company, created special film for movies.

In the early 20th century, the movie business grew in the United States. Several small movie companies moved west from New York City to Los Angeles in the

Films during the first decades of the 20th century were silent and black-and-white. This still from the 1928 silent film *The Cameraman* stars U.S. actor and director Buster Keaton (left).

early 1920s. These movie pioneers helped build what became Hollywood. Many of the production companies they started are still successful today. These companies include Universal Studios, Warner Brothers, and Metro-Goldwyn-Mayer (MGM).

As Hollywood grew, **filmmakers** thought about ways to make movies better. Through the early part of the 20th century, movies were all silent films. Then, filmmakers used new sound technology to bring music and conversation to movies. Attendance at movie theaters climbed to record highs. People from all over wanted to see these new movies called "talkies." Talkies soon replaced silent films.

During the first half of the 20th century, color film was available, but it was very expensive. Most movies were filmed in black and white through the 1950s.

Today, we can watch movies on big screens and little screens, in movie theaters and at home. Movies have complex soundtracks. They also have advanced effects such as brilliant color and amazing computer graphics. Movies continue to light up the screen and fascinate audiences around the world.

21st Century Content

While American and European audiences fell in love with talkies, Japanese moviegoers enjoyed a combination of theater and movies. A narrator, called a *benshi*, stood next to the screen when a movie was playing. The benshi explained the action through voice, movement, and storytelling. Although sound technology was available, Japanese filmmakers continued to use benshis through the 1930s. The tradition is rooted in Japanese theater and shows how a country's culture can influence technology and art.

Behind the Scenes

Making a movie requires the labor, creativity, and ideas of many individuals working together. Different people are responsible for different parts of movie production. A screenwriter creates the script for the movie. The director decides how the movie will look and feel. The actors bring it to life. Costume designers and makeup artists give characters **authenticity**. Set designers create the look and feel of the setting of the movie. The cinematographer films the movie. Production companies oversee the entire process. They obtain funding and manage the day-to-day process of getting the movie made.

The moviemaking process is unique for each film. But it usually involves three stages. The first stage is called development, or pre-production. This is when the

The first step of making a movie is usually writing the screenplay. It is common for screenwriters to revise the script many times.

idea for the film comes together. A screenwriter writes several drafts of the script until it is ready. Actors are cast in various roles. Funding and locations for filming the movie are secured. This stage requires brainstorming, conversation, and writing. As the process continues, more technology and equipment become necessary.

Filming begins in the second stage, called production. Some movies are filmed on location, such as in a park or a specific building. Other movies are filmed on a set, which is a special place designed for filming movies. During production, cinematographers use movie cameras to shoot the scenes. These cameras need lots of bright light to record pictures. Some scenes can be difficult to film, such as car chases or underwater scenes. Cameras and other equipment can be easily damaged. To film these complicated scenes, cameras are placed in airtight boxes for protection.

Another piece of equipment on many sets is a boom, or a long stick. The boom holds a microphone or camera over the scene being filmed. Advances in equipment, cameras, and lights allow filmmakers to get more complicated shots. For example, filming a moving actor or vehicle is difficult. A dolly (a platform on wheels) is used to roll the camera along while following the actor or vehicle. This makes the process easier. In other cases, a special device attaches a camera to a helicopter to film a scene from above.

Some of the most important discoveries in film technology were in sound and audio recording. When talkies began, filmmakers ran into sound quality problems. Background sounds, such as cars honking and phones ringing, could sometimes be heard in early

Filming on-location water scenes in the 1975 thriller *Jaws* challenged the production crew. But the Oscar-winning movie was a huge hit at the box office.

movies. Filmmakers shifted most productions to special soundstages. On a soundstage, movies can be filmed without extra noise. As new kinds of recording devices and microphones became available, clearer and more **versatile** sound was achieved.

In the final stage of a movie, called post-production, a film is edited and prepared for viewing. In the early days, editors cut and pasted film together by hand. Special effects were often added during filming by using camera tricks, props, or models. Through the years, filmmakers

The 2002 film *Harry Potter and the Chamber of Secrets* has several scenes that include computer-generated effects.

have worked on making the post-production process easier and faster. Today, computer software and digital technology have made film editing better than ever. Computer technology allows filmmakers to do many things that couldn't be done before. For example, they can add special effects, such as monsters, with the use of computer-generated imagery.

Movie productions have come a long way since the early silent films and talkies. Today, moviemakers use everything from computer graphics to elaborate set designs to bring entertainment to people everywhere.

Life & Career Skills

Do you want to work in the movie industry? There are many different jobs to choose from. Depending on your interests and talents, you can act in movies or work behind the scenes. Unfortunately, there are usually fewer jobs than there are people who want them. Making movies is competitive, but people still head to Hollywood to follow their dreams. Whether you are interested in acting, writing, set design, or sound engineering, it is an exciting industry. To prepare, brush up on your collaboration skills. Making a movie is always a team effort.

CHAPTER THREE

Innovations in Movies

Smaller and lighter equipment has made it easier to film in remote locations.

Have you ever wondered how moviemaking has changed over the years? Two of the most important inspirations for innovative filmmaking are technology and culture.

Equipment can change how movies are made. New technologies allow filmmakers to do things they couldn't do years ago. World events and cultures can inspire filmmakers to create new styles of movies.

A director and crew film a silent movie in the summer of 1916 outside of New York City. The studio was a former greenhouse, so its interior had plenty of natural light.

Early filmmakers did not have the kinds of advanced technology that we have today. Many early films were made with simple sets, no special effects, and usually one camera angle. It wasn't until the early 1900s that new technology began to change the way movies are made. Many discoveries made back then still influence filmmakers today.

One early film pioneer was an Englishman named George Albert Smith. He created many new effects in movies. By filming over already exposed film, Smith

This still from the 1944 film *The Canterville Ghost* shows a double exposure, or ghost image. Englishman George Albert Smith is credited with developing the technique.

made what is thought to be the first double exposure, or ghost image, in a motion picture. He was also one of the first filmmakers to show a close-up, or enlarged view, of one part of a person or thing. These kinds of shots are very common in movies today, but were once groundbreaking for audiences.

Another early pioneer was a Frenchman named Georges Meliès. He made one important discovery by accident. His camera stopped, and he continued filming when it started up again. Meliès noticed that this stop-and-go filming made it look as if time were jumping forward. Soon after, in the United States, filmmaker Edwin Stanton Porter used a similar technique to tell stories with movies. Porter was one of the first people to edit together a **narrative** in a movie. These techniques allowed filmmakers to tie different events in a story together.

Recording technology brought some of the biggest changes to filmmaking. It allowed filmmakers to add music and **dialogue** to movies. *The Jazz Singer*, the first talkie, was released in 1927. This was just two years before the Great Depression. Talkies led to a popular new kind of movie—the musical. The lighthearted music and dancing of musicals helped to bring laughter and cheer to people during a difficult time in America's history. Other **genres** inspired by social conditions in America were gangster movies, westerns, and comedies.

Comedy has always been a part of movies. Early comedic stars, such as Charlie Chaplin and Harold Lloyd, mastered the complicated stunts and expressive gestures of slapstick common in silent movies. The invention of sound brought a new kind of comedy, full of fast-talking characters and wild adventures. Though the style of comedy has changed with the times, comedies remain popular today.

Writer, director, and actor Charlie Chaplin prepares to eat his boot in the 1925 silent film *The Gold Rush*.

Computer-animated films have grown by leaps and bounds. Today, computer-animated movies such as *Toy Story*, *Finding Nemo*, and *Monsters, Inc.* are huge box-office success stories.

Computer animators can create new images, characters, and imaginary worlds. Powerful computers and sophisticated 3-D computer programs allow computer animators to bring these images to life.

Technical advances aren't the only things that inspire filmmakers. Computer animators and filmmakers around the world are inspired by art, culture, history, and politics. The Indian filmmaker D. H. Phalke started a new kind of movie called the mythological. These are based on India's colorful stories. Chinese filmmakers, inspired by their country's Beijing Opera, created dramatic and exciting fight scenes. Inspirations from around the world continue to help filmmakers come up with new ideas.

Learning & Innovation Skills

How a director decides to look at, or frame, a particular scene affects how an audience will respond. Imagine you are a movie director trying to frame a shot. How will you show the action and emotion of the scene? Make a circle with your thumb and forefinger and hold it up to your eye. Look around. Move your circle close to your eye and then far away for different effects. Can you imagine all the ways a director must consider framing each shot in a movie?

CHAPTER FOUR

The Biz

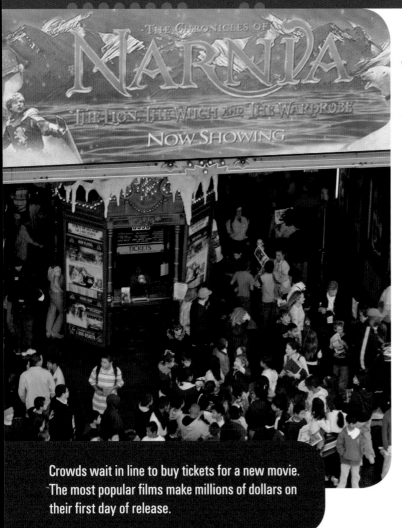

Crowds wait in line to buy tickets for a new movie. The most popular films make millions of dollars on their first day of release.

When the Lumiére brothers sent movies around the world, they expanded the market for their new product. They set the stage for movies to become a popular form of entertainment. Today, movies are a big business. Audiences around the world enjoy watching them. Successful movies can make a lot of money. But it also takes a lot of money to make a movie.

Hollywood, California, is home to some of the world's major film studios.

Hollywood, California, quickly became a hotspot for the movie business. The first Hollywood studios created a structure for making movies. Studio owners worked to find ways to make as many movies as they could. They also looked for ways to keep costs down. The structure they came up with was known as the studio system. Movies were made in phases, much like a car or toy is manufactured. Today, production companies use a similar structure for making movies. This structure provides many different kinds of jobs.

Another important innovation of early Hollywood was the star system. While Hollywood was growing, production companies needed people to bring attention to their movies. These companies decided to focus on particular actors and actresses. They created elaborate stories about and glamorous photographs of their young actors and actresses. In doing so, they created the first movie stars. Soon, audiences wanted to see more movies featuring their favorite stars.

Today, movie stars aren't just seen in films. We see photographs of movie stars on television, billboards, and on the Internet. Stars are often hired to sell products, such as perfume or clothing. Sometimes they help raise money for important causes. We see images of movie stars doing what seem to be everyday activities, such as shopping or having lunch. It is important to remember that much of what is written about them is carefully created.

The movie industry provides opportunities for those willing to take a chance. Many Jewish immigrants, who had been forced to flee their countries during World War II,

Some movie stars get involved in causes that affect them personally. Actor Michael J. Fox (right) and his wife and son attend a benefit for the Michael J. Fox Foundation for Parkinson's Research.

found success in early Hollywood. African American filmmaker Oscar Micheaux made more than 40 movies between 1919 and 1948. Micheaux found creative ways

21st Century Content

 Some filmmakers specialize in showing us life from a certain point of view. For example, African American director Spike Lee makes movies about young black characters in urban neighborhoods. The movies of Spanish director Pedro Almodóvar celebrate unusual choices and strong female characters. Digital movie cameras allow people around the world to produce movies that show us diverse characters, styles, and points of view. Many amateur filmmakers create their own films and upload them to Web sites such as YouTube. There, the films can be viewed by anyone with Internet access.

to finance them by selling small shares to individuals in African American communities. Although men often held powerful positions in early Hollywood, women also took leading roles both on and off the screen. For example, Canadian film producer Mary Sennett produced more than 1,000 films through her company, Keystone. Today, the movie industry continues to provide opportunities for many people.

CHAPTER FIVE

Showstoppers and Innovators

The movie industry wouldn't be as big as it is today without the talents of so many people. Here are just a few who have made big contributions.

Mary Pickford

Mary Pickford was one of the world's first movie stars. She was a silent movie actress and the highest paid woman in the world at the time. She was also a skilled businesswoman. In 1919,

Mary Pickford was a producer, director, and actress. In 1929, she won the first Academy Award given to an actress for a role in a talking picture.

she started a production company called United Artists with successful director D. W. Griffith, famous comedian Charlie Chaplin, and her husband, actor Douglas Fairbanks. United Artists continues to this day.

Buster Keaton

Buster Keaton was one of the most inventive filmmakers in history. He made numerous short and feature-length films over the course of his career. In one of his first movies, he played all the members of a small theater company. Posing as the actors, musicians, and audience members, he filmed one scene right on top of the next. This was a new and creative form of moviemaking. Keaton's **exacting** style meant that he did everything possible to make each movie the best it could be. He would perform his own charming, funny, and often dangerous stunts. He also rigged elaborate special effects, such as a real train crash.

Alfred Hitchcock

British-born director Alfred Hitchcock was a master of thriller and suspense movies. His name has become synonymous with suspense. Dramatic light and shadows, slow shots, and dizzying angles are trademarks of his unique style. The broad popularity of his many movies has made him one of the most famous movie directors in the world.

Alfred Hitchcock talks with actor Tippi Hedren during the filming of *The Birds* in 1963. Other famous Hitchcock films include *Rear Window* (1954), *Vertigo* (1958), and *Psycho* (1960).

Steven Spielberg and George Lucas

Steven Spielberg and George Lucas are two very famous American filmmakers. Spielberg has achieved worldwide fame. Three of his films, *Jaws*, *E.T. The Extra-Terrestrial*, and *Jurassic Park*, set records for making more

Directors Steven Spielberg (left) and George Lucas attend an awards ceremony in Beverly Hills, California, in 2002.

money than any other films that came before them.

Lucas created the *Star Wars* series and founded Lucasfilms. He also founded an animation company that later became Pixar.

The two men collaborated to create the great *Indiana Jones* adventure films. Both Academy Award–winning directors are known for their innovative special effects, and both have won the Visual Effect Society's Lifetime Achievement award.

Learning & Innovation Skills

If you were to make a movie, what would it be about? Would you tell a real story, such as a documentary of your life and community? Or would you create fiction—a thriller, a fantasy, or a comedy? Write about the movie you would make. What would your movie be about? Who would play the various roles? Where would you film it? The ending of a movie is often what audiences remember most. How will your movie end? Try imagining it with different endings, and see which one you like the best. Then pick up a camera. You're ready for those three famous words, "Lights! Camera! Action!"

Glossary

authenticity (aw-then-TIH-suh-tee) the quality of being genuine or real

dialogue (DYE-uh-lawg) the conversation or talking in a movie or play

documentary (dah-kyuh-MEN-tuh-ree) a movie or television program that presents factual information

exacting (eg-ZAKT-ing) extremely detailed or precise

filmmakers (FILM-make-uhrz) people who make, create, or produce films

genres (JON-ruhz) categories of expression based on form, content, or style

industry (IN-duh-stree) a kind of business or commerce

narrative (NA-ruh-tiv) story or tale

versatile (VUR-suh-tuhl) able to be used or to move in different ways; flexible

For More Information

BOOKS

Buckley, Annie. *Making Movies*. Mankato, MN: Child's World, 2006.

O'Brien, Lisa. *Lights, Camera, Action! Making Movies and TV from the Inside Out*. Toronto: Maple Tree Press, 2007.

WEB SITES

Yahoo! Kids - Movies
kids.yahoo.com/movies
Access a database with information on hundreds of films, and find out what's playing at a theater near you.

YouthLearn
kidsvid.altec.org/making.html
Learn some tricks that will help you make movies that will impress your audience

Index

About the Author

Annie Buckley is a writer, artist, and children's book author who lives and works in Los Angeles. Growing up near Hollywood, Annie remembers passing the gates of Paramount Studios on her way to school and going with her family to see the stars on Hollywood Boulevard. She enjoys watching romantic comedies and foreign movies.